Pebble®

I DON'T BULLY

I Am Respectful

by Melissa Higgins

Consulting Editor: Gail Saunders-Smith, PhD

Content Consultant: Susan M. Swearer, PhD
Professor of School Psychology and Licensed
Psychologist; Co-Director, Bullying Research Network
University of Nebraska–Li

T0052267

CAPSTONE PRESS
a capstone imprint

Pebble Books are published by Capstone Press,
1710 Roe Crest Drive, North Mankato, Minnesota 56003
www.capstonepub.com

Copyright © 2014 by Capstone Press, a Capstone imprint. All rights reserved.
No part of this publication may be reproduced in whole or in part, or stored in a retrieval system, or transmitted in any form or by any means, electronic, mechanical, photocopying, recording, or otherwise, without written permission of the publisher.

Library of Congress Cataloging-in-Publication Data
Higgins, Melissa, 1953–
I am respectful / by Melissa Higgins.
pages cm.—(Pebble books. I don't bully)
Summary: "Simple text and full color photographs describe how to be respectful, not a bully"—Provided by publisher.
Includes bibliographical references and index.
Audience: Age 5–8.
Audience: K to grade 3.
ISBN 978-1-4765-4067-2 (library binding)
ISBN 978-1-4765-5171-5 (paperback)
ISBN 978-1-4765-6036-6 (ebook pdf)
1. Respect—Juvenile literature. I. Title.
BJ1533.R4H54 2015
179'.9—dc23 2013029994

Note to Parents and Teachers

The I Don't Bully set supports national curriculum standards for social studies related to people and cultures. This book describes being respectful. The images support early readers in understanding the text. The repetition of words and phrases helps early readers learn new words. This book also introduces early readers to subject-specific vocabulary words, which are defined in the Glossary section. Early readers may need assistance to read some words and to use the Table of Contents, Glossary, Read More, Internet Sites, and Index sections of the book.

Printed in the United States 5973

Table of Contents

I Am Polite 5
I Like Differences 13
I Am Calm 17
I Think about Others 21

Glossary 22
Read More 23
Internet Sites 23
Index 24

Champ

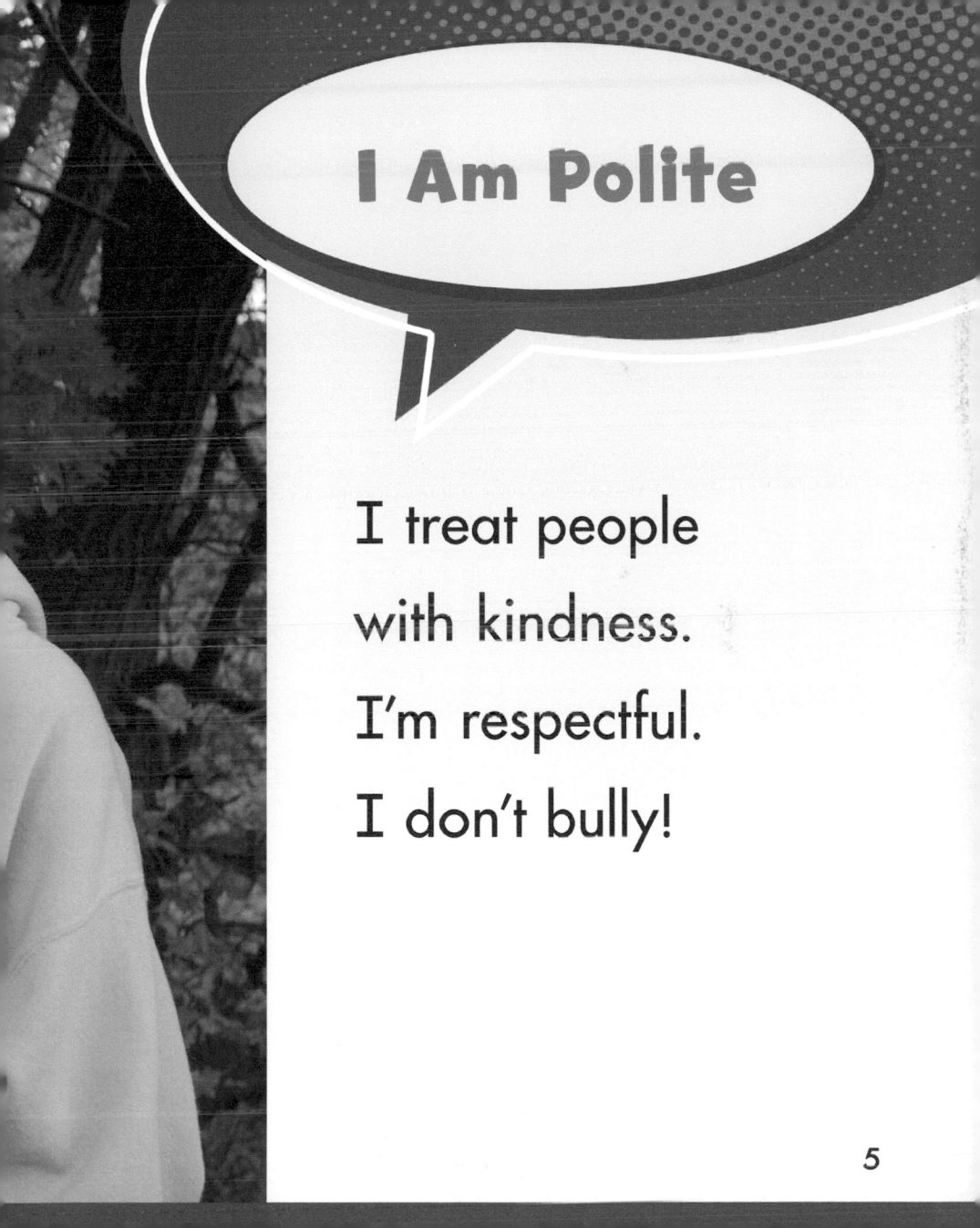

I Am Polite

I treat people
with kindness.
I'm respectful.
I don't bully!

BRAIN TEASER!
Level A
Morgan
Melissa
Aisha
Cullen
Taylor
TILE TEASER #2
28

I'm a good listener.
Kids who bully
don't care what
others have to say.

STATUTE

I'm courteous and
respect people's space.
Kids who bully hit and
shove to get their way.

Family Food Drive

I use good manners when I speak. Kids who bully hurt people's feelings with rude words and gestures.

I Like Differences

I like all kinds of people.
Kids who bully tease
people who don't look
like they do.

I like learning about other beliefs. Kids who bully make fun of people with different beliefs.

Respect your classmate's artwork.
You decide how to solve the problem
Be kind and use kind words.

I Am Calm

I find peaceful ways to let out anger. Kids who bully have tantrums. They don't care who they hurt.

I can disagree without getting angry. Kids who bully yell and fight when they disagree.

I Think about Others

I treat other people
how I want to be treated.
I never want to be bullied.
So I will never be a bully!

Glossary

bully—to be mean to someone else over and over again

gesture—a movement that communicates a feeling or an idea

manners—polite behavior; people who use good manners are kind to other people

peaceful—calm

respectful—to treat others in a way that shows respect for them

rude—not polite

tantrum—burst of anger

Read More

Joseph, Kurt. *I Am Respectful.* Kids of Character. New York: Gareth Stevens Pub., 2011.

Meiners, Cheri J. *Cool Down and Work Through Anger.* Learning to Get Along. Minneapolis: Free Spirit Pub., 2010.

Rissman, Rebecca. *Should Theo Say Thank You?: Being Respectful.* What Would You Do? Chicago: Capstone Heinemann Library, 2013.

Internet Sites

FactHound offers a safe, fun way to find Internet sites related to this book. All of the sites on FactHound have been researched by our staff.

Here's all you do:

Visit *www.facthound.com*

Type in this code: 9781476540672

Index

anger, 17
beliefs, 15
courtesy, 8
differences, 13, 15
disagreeing, 19
fighting, 19
hitting, 9
kindness, 5
listening, 7
manners, 11
shoving, 9
teasing, 13

Word Count: 148
Grade: 1
Early-Intervention Level: 13

Editorial Credits
Jeni Wittrock, editor; Juliette Peters, designer; Svetlana Zhurkin, media researcher; Kathy McColley, production specialist; Sarah Schuette, photo stylist; Marcy Morin, photo scheduler

Photo Credits
Capstone Studio/Karon Dubke